HISTO CORN

Vikings

Alice Harman

Explore the world with Popcorn - your complete first non-fiction library.

Look out for more titles in the Popcorn range. All books have the same format of simple text and striking images. Text is carefully matched to the pictures to help readers to identify and understand key vocabulary.
www.waylandbooks.co.uk/popcorn

Published in 2013 by Wayland
Copyright © Wayland 2013

Wayland
Hachette Children's Books
338 Euston Road
London NW1 3BH

Wayland Australia
Level 17/207 Kent Street
Sydney NSW 2000

Produced for Wayland by
White-Thomson Publishing Ltd
www.wtpub.co.uk
+44 (0)843 208 7460

Editor: Alice Harman
Designer: Clare Nicholas
Picture researcher: Alice Harman
Series consultant: Kate Ruttle
Design concept: Paul Cherrill

British Library Cataloguing in Publication Data
Harman, Alice.
  Vikings. -- (History corner)(Popcorn)
  1. Vikings--Juvenile literature. 2. Civilization, Viking--
  Juvenile literature.
  I. Title II. Series
  948'.022-dc23

  ISBN: 978 0 7502 7810 2

10 9 8 7 6 5 4 3 2 1

Wayland is a division of Hachette Children's Books,
an Hachette UK company.
www.hachette.co.uk

Printed and bound in China

Picture/illustration credits: Alamy: Photos 12 5, Mary Evans Picture Library 6, 7, Rob Watkins 9, All Canada Photos 10, Richard Peel 14; Peter Bull: 23; Stefan Chabluk: 4; Corbis: Heritage Images 8, Tim Thompson 11, PoodlesRock 12, Werner Forman Archive 15, National Geographic Society 16; Shutterstock: Alvaro Cabrera Jimenez 22; TopFoto: The Granger Collection 13; Werner Forman Archive: Statens Historiska Museum 17; Wikimedia: 21

Every effort has been made to clear copyright. Should there be any inadvertent omission, please apply to the publisher for rectification.

# Contents

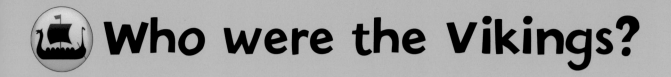# Who were the Vikings?

The Vikings came from northern
Europe. They travelled to many parts
of Europe, Asia and North America.

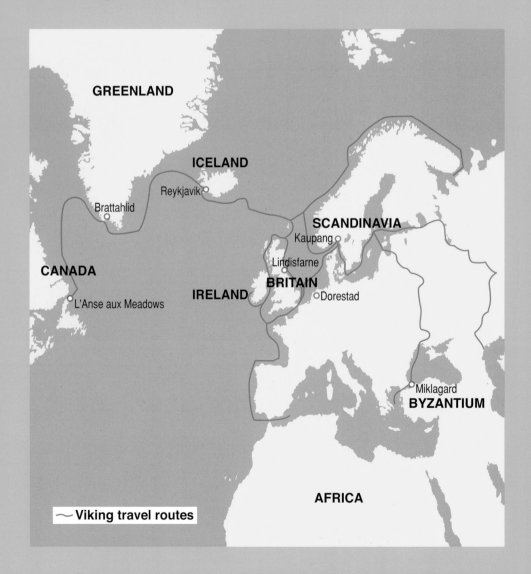

GREENLAND

ICELAND

Reykjavik

Brattahlid

SCANDINAVIA

Kaupang

Lindisfarne

CANADA

BRITAIN

IRELAND

Dorestad

L'Anse aux Meadows

Miklagard

BYZANTIUM

AFRICA

~ **Viking travel routes**

The Vikings lived between
1,300 and 900 years ago.
They were great explorers,
traders and warriors.

Vikings sailed across the sea in huge
wooden boats called longships.

🚢 Viking leaders

Erik the Red was a famous Viking explorer and leader. His son, Leif Erikson, was also an explorer, who discovered North America.

Erik was called 'Red' because of his bright red hair and beard.

Cnut the Great was a Viking king who lived around 1,000 years ago. He ruled over Denmark, England, Norway and parts of Sweden.

In a famous story, Cnut showed his people that, although he was a powerful king, he could not control the sea.

Cnut the Great was also called King Canute.

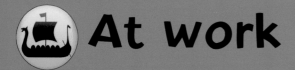 # At work

Viking blacksmiths made strong objects out of metal. These included the helmets and weapons that warriors took into battle.

This wooden carving shows a blacksmith mending a man's sword.

Women looked after the home and the children. They often ran the family farms while their husbands were away on long journeys.

These women are dressed up as Vikings to show people how Viking women made clothes from sheep's wool.

Some women went to war to care for ill and hurt soldiers.

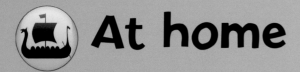 At home

Vikings built their houses from wood, stones and mud. They often put grass on the roofs to keep the houses warm.

Most people in the countryside lived in longhouses.

Most longhouses had one long space inside. The people lived at one end of the house, and their animals lived at the other end. It could get quite smelly!

People kept warm by sitting around a big fire in the middle of the house.

Viking houses didn't have windows, so it was very dark inside.

fire pit

Food and drink

Families grew crops, and kept animals for meat and cheese. They also collected nuts and berries, and caught fish.

Rich Vikings rode powerful horses when they went hunting.

Men used dogs to hunt large animals, such as deer or bears.

On special occasions, Vikings had a
drink called mead. This was made
of honey. People drank it out of
wooden cups or long drinking horns.

Drinking horns were made
of cow horns that were
decorated with silver or gold.

Clothes and jewellery

The Vikings kept warm in cold weather by wearing layers of thick clothes. These were made of wool and animal skins.

These people are dressed in Viking clothes.

Men and women wore silver or gold jewellery, such as necklaces, bracelets and brooches. Viking jewellery was often large and heavy.

Some people wore armlets, like this decorated silver one, on their upper arm.

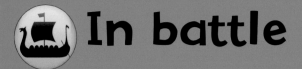In battle

The Vikings were famous for being fierce warriors. They often attacked people who did not want to fight. They stole expensive objects, and sold people as slaves.

This painting shows the Vikings attacking Christian people in Ireland.

Rich Vikings wore metal helmets when they were fighting. These protected their heads from being badly hurt. Poor Vikings wore hats made of leather.

The most expensive helmets were decorated with patterns and pictures.

From evidence people have found, we know that Viking helmets did not have horns.

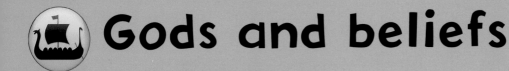 Gods and beliefs

Thor was the Viking god of thunder. The Vikings believed that he ruled the skies, and was very strong and brave. He travelled in a chariot pulled by two goats.

Thor had a magical hammer that returned to his hand when he threw it in battle.

The Vikings believed that when a warrior died in battle, he went to a place called Valhalla. This was a great hall where dead warriors ate and drank as much as they wanted.

The god Odin sat in a huge chair in Valhalla, with a wolf on each side of him.

Odin

Fun and games

A board game called hnefatafl
was often played in Viking times.
It may have been played with dice,
but people today are not sure.

The pieces used to play hnefatafl were
carved from wood or stone.

The Vikings loved telling and hearing stories and poems. These were often about gods, or Viking leaders and people from the past.

Long Viking stories about the past are called 'sagas'.

Brünnhilde was a famous and powerful character in Viking sagas.

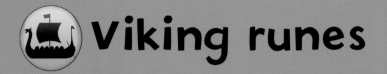

Viking runes

The Vikings wrote using pictures called runes. There were 24 runes, and each stood for a letter or sound.

This alphabet shows how Viking runes match up with the letters and sounds we use today.

Can you work out what English word these Viking runes spell out?

Answer: pen

f	u	th	a	r	k
g	w	h	n	i	z
s	t	b	y	el	p
e	m	l	ng	d	o

Spell out other words in runes. Ask your friends to work out what they say.

Bake Viking bread

You will need:
- 360g (13oz) wholewheat flour
- 250g (9oz) white flour
- 1 tsp baking soda · 1 tsp salt
- 475ml (17fl oz) warm water
- 90g (3oz) oats

Vikings ate simple, heavy bread that filled them up during long journeys. Make some bread, and taste it for yourself!

1. Mix all the dry ingredients in a bowl, except for a quarter of the oats. Mix in the water, until it gets difficult to stir the mixture.

2. Push the mixture about with your fingers, until it becomes stiff. Take the mixture out of the bowl, and place it on a flat surface.

3. Use your hands to make the mixture into a round shape. Place it on a baking tray. Sprinkle the rest of the oats on top.

4. Put the baking tray into a cold oven. Ask an adult to turn the oven to 375°C (190°F/ Gas Mark 5). Bake the bread for one hour. Yummy!

Glossary

armlet a band worn around the upper part of the arm

battle a fight between two big groups of people

chariot a small cart that is pulled by animals

Christian people who follow the religion of Christianity, and believe in Jesus

crops plants grown for food, either for people or animals

dice six-sided cubes with different numbers of dots on each side, which are used for playing games

explorer someone who travels to unknown places

horns hard, bony parts on the heads of some animals, such as cows or goats

hunt to chase and catch animals for food

longhouse a type of long-sided house in which Viking families lived

slave someone who has to work for no money, and is not free

thunder the loud, rumbling noise heard during a storm

warrior an experienced soldier or fighter

weapon an object, such as a sword, that is used for fighting

Index